The Ultim Cream Recipes for Everyone

Simple and Easy Preparation for Pure Pleasure

BY: Valeria Ray

License Notes

A Special Reward for Purchasing My Book!

Thank you, cherished reader, for purchasing my book and taking the time to read it. As a special reward for your decision, I would like to offer a gift of free and discounted books directly to your inbox. All you need to do is fill in the box below with your email address and name to start getting amazing offers in the comfort of your own home. You will never miss an offer because a reminder will be sent to you. Never miss a deal and get great deals without having to leave the house! Subscribe now and start saving!

https://valeria-ray.gr8.com

Contents

Simple and Easy Ice Cream Recipes

MMMMMMMMMMMMMMMMMMMMMMMMMMMM

(1) Cotton Candy

This cotton candy ice cream might be a hit with kids – and you! Delve into the flavours of the circus, or a carnival in a sweet, cool treat. Make separate batches of different colours and mix and match servings to make this ice cream even more fun.

Yield: 2 pints

Cooking Time: 10 minutes

List of Ingredients:

- 4 cups of ice cream base, without vanilla
- 1 tsp. of Cotton Candy extract / flavour
- Blue food colouring

MMMMMMMMMMMMMMMMMMMMMMMMMMMMMM

Instructions:

1. Combine all of the ingredients. Add food colouring in 1 – 2 drop increments until desired colour is achieved. Light, pastel colours are best!

2. Adjust to desired taste.

3. Pour into an air tight container and freeze for at least 6 hours.

(2) Lemon

This simple lemon ice cream is sweet but tangy. It is citrusy and refreshing. It is the perfect mix of sweet, sour and creamy.

Yield: 2 pints

Cooking Time: 10 minutes

List of Ingredients:

- 4 cups of ice cream base, without vanilla
- ¾ cup of lemon juice, chilled
- 5 tsp. of fresh lemon zest, finely grated
- 1 – 2 drops of yellow food colouring (Optional)

MMMMMMMMMMMMMMMMMMMMMMMMMMMMMMM

Instructions:

1. Combine all of the ingredients. Add food colouring until a very light-yellow colour is achieved.

2. Adjust to desired taste. Add more lemon juice if a stronger flavour is desired.

3. Pour into an air tight container and freeze for at least 6 hours.

(3) Coffee

Coffee doesn't only have to be your morning pick me up. Infusing your favourite brew in a creamy ice cream base is just as delicious as your cup of joe in the morning – maybe even more. You can add nuts, shredded coconut, mini chocolate chips or even cookies to this mixture. Have fun with it!

Yield: 2 pints

Cooking Time: 10 minutes

List of Ingredients:

- 4 cups of ice cream base, with vanilla
- ¼ cup of hot water
- 2 tbsp. of instant coffee
- 1 tbsp. of condensed milk

MMMMMMMMMMMMMMMMMMMMMMMMMMMMMM

Instructions:

1. Dissolve instant coffee into hot water. Allow to cool completely.

2. Mix coffee and condensed milk. Pour this mixture into the ice cream base and combine all of the ingredients.

3. Adjust to desired taste. Add more coffee if a stronger flavour is desired.

4. Pour into an air tight container and freeze for at least 6 hours.

(4) Vanilla

Nothing beats the classic. Vanilla ice cream doesn't require an ice cream maker and is simple and delicious. You can enjoy it as is, top it with some of your favourite toppings such a fruit, nuts melted chocolate or caramel sauce or use it as a base for more flavour variations.

Yield: 4 pints (about 12 cups)

Cooking Time: 10 minutes

List of Ingredients:

- 4 cups of heavy whipping cream, cold
- 4 cups of sweetened condensed milk, cold
- 4 tsp. of vanilla extract
- 2 vanilla bean pods, seeds

MMMMMMMMMMMMMMMMMMMMMMMMMMMMMM

Instructions:

1. Whip the cold whipping cream until soft peaks are formed.

2. Add condensed milk and continue whipping until stiff peaks are formed.

3. Stir vanilla extract and seeds into mixture.

4. Scoop mixture into an air-tight container and freeze for at least 6 hours. Preferably overnight.

**Can be stored in the freezer for up to 6 weeks.

**Will be required as the base for other recipes in this book (without vanilla). Steps 1 – 3.

(5) Homemade Caramel Sauce

This homemade caramel sauce is perfect to drizzle over your favourite ice cream flavours or even be swirled into some of them – I recommend the vanilla and cookies and cream flavours.

Yield: 1 cup

Cooking time: 10 minutes

List of Ingredients:

- 4 tbsp. of butter, room temperature
- ½ cup of granulated sugar
- ½ cup of heavy cream
- ½ tsp. of cinnamon

MMMMMMMMMMMMMMMMMMMMMMMMMMMMMM

Instructions:

1. Melt butter over medium heat in a small heavy-bottom saucepan.

2. Add sugar and heavy cream to the mixture with a wooden spoon or rubber spatula.

3. Allow the mixture to boil without stirring. Boil for 4 to 5 minutes. Do not wait for the caramel sauce to thicken over the heat, it will thicken as it cools.

4. Remove the sauce from the heat and stir in the cinnamon. Transfer the caramel sauce to a glass container to cool.

**Use a wet brush to brush down sugar crystals from the sides of the pot as the mixture boils.

(6) Vanilla (Dairy Free)

This version of vanilla ice cream is made with coconut milk and it is simply delicious. For those of you who choose not to or cannot consume animal dairy, this version is delicious on its own and it is a great option for the bases needed in this book, so you can enjoy these recipes!

Yield: 4 pints

Cooking Time: 30 – 40 minutes

List of Ingredients:

- 4 cans of full fat coconut milk (13.5oz)
- 1 can of coconut cream (13.5oz)
- 2 ½ cups of sugar
- 5 tsp. of vanilla

MMMMMMMMMMMMMMMMMMMMMMMMMMMMMMM

Instructions:

1. Mix 4 cans of room temperature coconut milks with sugar. Pour mixture into a saucepan on medium-low heat. Allow to simmer for about 30 minutes, until milk is thick, and the volume has been reduced. (The milk will turn a golden colour).

2. Once thick, remove from heat and allow to cool completely.

3. Whip coconut cream until light and fluffy. Add, cooled coconut milk mixture and whip until stiff.

4. Place in an air tight container and freeze for 4 hours.

**Allow to sit at room temperature for 2 minutes before scooping.

(7) Ice Cream Cake

This is a great dessert for a group of people. The cake is soft and moist, and the ice cream is creamy and amazing. The frosting can be whipped cream or melted chocolate, either one is delicious! You can add nuts, sprinkles, cookies, marshmallows or candy to the top of your ice cream cake. You can mix up flavours as well; cookies and cream, chocovanilla, chocolate almond, strawberry vanilla... or even add 2 f flavours of ice cream – the possibilities are endless.

Yield:

Cooking Time:

List of Ingredients:

- 3 cups of vanilla ice cream
- 1 box of cake / brownie mix – eggs, oil and water needed according to package directions
- 2 cups of whipped topping

MMMMMMMMMMMMMMMMMMMMMMMMMMM

Instructions:

1. Prepare box cake according to package directions. Allow to cool completely. Freeze overnight.

2. Allow ice cream to sit for 3 minutes before adding it to cake. This will make it spread easier. Take the cake out of the freezer and spread ice cream in an even layer over cake.

3. Scoop whipped topping onto ice cream layer and spread evenly.

4. Freeze again for 1 – 2 hours.

(8) Chocolate

Hello chocolate lovers! This flavour is perfect for those who like a slightly bitter, savoury ice cream. Add mini chocolate chips, marshmallows, almonds or whatever your heart desires to the mixture and enjoy your chocolate fix. Double the chocolate and top with chocolate syrup.

Yield: 4 pints (about 12 cups)

Cooking Time: 10 minutes

List of Ingredients:

- 4 cups of heavy whipping cream, cold
- 4 cups of sweetened condensed milk, cold
- 4 tsp. of vanilla extract (optional)
- 2 ½ cups of bittersweet chocolate

MMMMMMMMMMMMMMMMMMMMMMMMMMMMMMMM

Instructions:

1. Whip the cold whipping cream until soft peaks are formed.

2. Add condensed milk and continue whipping until stiff peaks are formed.

3. Stir vanilla extract into mixture.

4. Spoon some of the ice cream base into the melted chocolate then quickly add chocolate mixture to the remaining base.

5. Scoop mixture into an air-tight container and freeze for at least 6 hours. Preferably overnight.

**Can be stored in the freezer for up to 6 weeks.

(9) Non-Fried Fried Ice Cream

Fried ice cream takes some time to master. But if you want to that crunchy coating on a scoop of ice cream, you don't need be a fried ice cream expert. Here's a delicious alternative that's just as good. Top with whipped cream and drizzle with caramel or chocolate syrup to make it even better.

Yield: 4

Cooking Time: 10 minutes

List of Ingredients:

- 4 scoops of vanilla ice cream
- 2 ½ cup of corn flakes, crushed finely
- 1 tbsp. of granulated sugar
- 1 tsp. of cinnamon
- 1 tbsp. of butter
- Whipped cream, sprinkles, maraschino cherries for garnish

MMMMMMMMMMMMMMMMMMMMMMMMMMMMMM

Instructions:

1. Place scoops of ice cream on a try and freeze until solid. About 1 hour.

2. Preheat oven to 350 degrees F.

3. Mix corn flakes, sugar and cinnamon together. Add butter and combine well.

4. Put on a small parchment lines baking sheet and bake for about 3 – 5 minutes, until corn flakes are toasted. Allow mixture to cool completely.

5. Remove scoops of ice cream from the freezer and roll each in the corn flakes mixture, make sure to coat all sides.

6. Re-freeze the covered ice cream scoops for at least 2 hours.

(10) Neapolitan

Neapolitan ice cream may not be something you thought you could make at home, but literally it's as easy as 1-2-3. All you have to do is put three flavours together and you have a delicious Strawberry-Vanilla-Chocolate ice cream!

Yield: 2 pints

Cooking Time: 10 minutes

List of Ingredients:

- 4 cups of ice cream base, with vanilla
- ½ cup of pureed frozen strawberries
- ½ cup of melted chocolate

MMMMMMMMMMMMMMMMMMMMMMMMMMMMMMM

Instructions:

1. Separate ice cream base into 3 separate equal parts.

2. Add the strawberry puree to one part in a bowl and fold until combined.

3. Add the melted chocolate to another part in a bowl and fold until well combined.

4. To create the traditional three colour look, you can add each flavour to an air tight container in layers, one on top of the other or you can alternate between flavours, being careful not to mix them.

5. Freeze for at least 6 hours.

(11) Ice Cream Cookie Sandwich

Scoop your favourite ice cream flavour between two large chocolate chip cookies and enjoy the amazing experience! These cookies are chewy and delightful. The cookie breaks off and compliments the cold ice cream perfectly. You can add sprinkles, nuts, chocolate chips, marshmallows and more to the sides of the ice cream to increase flavour and aesthetic.

Yield: 8 ice cream sandwiches

Cooking Time: 10 minutes

List of Ingredients:

- 1 – 2 ½ cups of vanilla ice cream
- ¼ cup of butter
- 1 cup of all-purpose flour
- ½ cup of brown sugar
- ¼ cup white sugar
- 1 egg
- ½ tsp. of vanilla
- ½ cup of peanut butter
- 1 tsp. of baking soda
- Pinch of salt
- ¼ cup of mini chocolate chips

MMMMMMMMMMMMMMMMMMMMMMMMMMMMM

Instructions:

1. Preheat your oven to 350 degrees F. Grease cookie sheet.

2. Sift together flour, salt and baking soda. Then cream together the butter and sugar.

3. Combine flour mixture, butter and sugar, peanut butter, vanilla and egg. Add chocolate chips and fold into the mixture.

4. Scoop cookie dough into hands, roll into a ball and place on cookie sheet. Leave about 2 inches of space between each ball.

5. Bake for 10 – 12 minutes, until edges of cookies are brown.

6. Cool completely.

7. Once cookies are completely cool, scoop ice cream onto 1 cookie and top with a second cookie to make a sandwich. Slightly press down to spread the ice cream evenly.

8. Freeze for no less than 2 hours, until ice cream is firm.

(12) Peanut Butter and Chocolate

Peanut Butter and Chocolate go great together in any form, and this ice cream flavour is no exception. This flavour is sweet yet savoury and salty. Use chunky peanut butter for a little crunch.

Yield: 2 pints

Cooking Time: 10 minutes

List of Ingredients:

- 4 cups of ice cream base, without vanilla
- 1 cup of peanut butter
- ½ cup of chocolate, melted and cool

MMMMMMMMMMMMMMMMMMMMMMMMMMMMMMM

Instructions:

1. Combine peanut butter, chocolate and base. Mix well.

2. Taste and adjust for flavour.

3. Freeze in an airtight container for at least 6 hours.

**Can be kept in the freezer for up to 2 weeks.

(13) Ice Cream Pie

This ice cream pie is perfect for gatherings where multiple people need dessert. The crust is chocolatey, crunchy and delicious. You can use whatever ice cream filling you want and top this pie with some sprinkles, cookie crumbs, crushed chocolate candy or caramel sauce.

Yield: 8 - 10

Cooking Time: 2 hours

List of Ingredients:

- 1 ½ cups of finely ground chocolate cookie crumbs
- 6 tbsp. of melted butter
- 2 pints of vanilla ice cream (See vanilla ice cream recipe)

MMMMMMMMMMMMMMMMMMMMMMMMMMMMMM

Instructions:

1. Remove the ice cream from the freezer and allow to soften slightly for a few minutes.

2. Mix cookie crumbs and melted butter together.

3. Press the mixture into a pie plate. Freeze for 1 hour.

4. Scoop ice cream into crust and spread out evenly. Cover with foil and freeze for 4 hours.

5. Serve with caramel sauce and your favourite toppings.

(14) Cookies and Cream

This is my personal favourite and if you like your ice cream with a little crunch and texture, it'll be yours too. This homemade no churn cookies and cream ice cream is an amazing dessert and doesn't take a lot to make.

Yield: 2 pints

Cooking Time: 10 minutes

List of Ingredients:

- 4 cups of ice cream base, with vanilla
- 16 chocolate cookies with cream filling

MMMMMMMMMMMMMMMMMMMMMMMMMMMMMMMM

Instructions:

1. Place cookies in a large Ziploc or storage bag. Use something heavy to crush the cookies into pieces. Do not completely crush cookies, you want to have pieces of different sizes.

2. Fold cookies into ice cream base.

3. Transfer to an air tight container and freeze for at least 6 hours.

(15) Ice Cream Cones

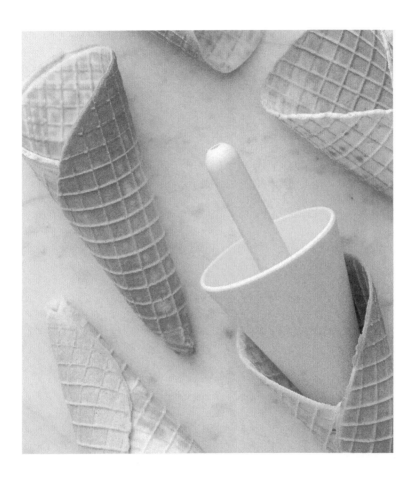

A scoop of ice cream definitely tastes better on an ice cream cone. You can make ice cream cones at home and with a little practice, you'll fast become an expert! Make them plain or dip in some chocolate after they have cooled and sprinkle with toppings such as nuts or sprinkles. Add melted chocolate to the batter to make a chocolate cone.

Serving: 16 cones

Cooking Time: 10 minutes

List of Ingredients:

- 1 ½ cups of all-purpose flour, sifted
- 1 cup of sugar
- 4 egg whites
- 6 tbsp. of milk
- 4 tbsp. of butter, melted
- 1 tsp. of vanilla
- A pinch of salt

MMMMMMMMMMMMMMMMMMMMMMMMMMMM

Instructions:

1. Whisk together sugar, milk, vanilla, salt and egg whites.

2. Stir in flour and butter until smooth.

3. Warm a medium skillet or frying pan on low heat.

4. This is where you will start to work quickly. Pour 1 ½ - 2 tbsp. of batter into pot and spread to make a thin even round layer.

5. Cook for 3 – 5 minutes and flip and cook on the other side for 1 – 2 minutes.

6. Remove disc and quickly and carefully roll it into a loose cone. Adjust the top to make it wider.

7. Hold the cone down on a flat surface for 1 – 2 minutes until it cools and hardens.

**Have someone help you out to make this easier.

**Roll cone from the bottom and then shape the cone.

(16) Rocky Road

Rocky road ice cream is definitely a favourite of mine. All of the ingredients o so well together and it is amazing. It's packed with marshmallows, almonds and chocolate.

Yield: 2 pints

Cooking Time: 5 minutes

List of Ingredients:

- 4 cups of ice cream base, with vanilla
- 1 cup of melted chocolate
- 1 cup of mini marshmallows
- 1 cup of almonds, toasted and chopped

MMMMMMMMMMMMMMMMMMMMMMMMMMMMMM

Instructions:

1. Combine ingredients. Swirl chocolate into ice cream base and gently fold in almonds and marshmallows.

2. Adjust to desired taste and texture

3. Freeze in an air tight container for at least 6 hours.

(17) Almond Cherry

This cherry ice cream is rich, full of flavour and texture. There are chunks of almonds and cherries throughout and it is simply delicious.

Yield: 2 pints

Cooking Time: 10 minutes

List of Ingredients:

- 4 cups of ice cream base, without vanilla
- 1 cup of frozen cherries, thawed, stoned and roughly chopped
- 3 – 5 tbsp. of cherry juice – taken from the thawed cherries
- ½ cup almonds, roughly chopped
- 2 tsp. of sugar

MMMMMMMMMMMMMMMMMMMMMMMMMMMMMM

Instructions:

1. Add sugar to a small bowl with thawed cherries. Mix to combine and allow to sit for 5 minutes.

2. Combine all of the ingredients. Mix the cherry juice into the ice cream base and fold almonds and cherries into ice cream base.

3. Adjust to desired taste.

4. Pour into an air tight container and freeze for at least 6 hours.

(18) S'mores

These campfire classics are just as delicious in ice cream form. This flavour has all of the classic ingredients of s'mores all swirled into a delicious vanilla ice cream base.

Yield: 2 pints

Cooking Time: 5 minutes

List of Ingredients:

- 4 cups of ice cream base, with vanilla
- 1 cup of chocolate, mini chocolate chips or chocolate bar roughly chopped
- ½ cup of marshmallow fluff
- 15 graham crackers, crushed

MMMMMMMMMMMMMMMMMMMMMMMMMMMMMMMM

Instructions:

1. Combine ingredients.

2. Adjust to desired taste and texture

3. Freeze in an air tight container for at least 6 hours.

(19) Mango

This tropical fruit has a sweet, distinct flavour that goes well with the milky base of ice cream. All you need is a few ingredients to enjoy a delicious tropical flavour.

Yield: 2 pints

Cooking Time: 10 minutes

List of Ingredients:

- 4 cups of ice cream base, with vanilla
- ½ cup of pureed frozen mango
- ½ tsp. of yellow food colouring (Optional)

MMMMMMMMMMMMMMMMMMMMMMMMMMMMMMM

Instructions:

1. Combine all of the ingredients. Add food colouring until desired colour is achieved.

2. Adjust to desired taste. Add more mango puree if a stronger flavour is desired.

3. Pour into an air tight container and freeze for at least 6 hours.

(20) Brown Sugar Bourbon

This flavour can be mastered in no time without an ice cream machine. The bourbon is mellowed out by the brown sugar, but it still has a wonderful bourbon flavour. This ice cream goes well with chopped pecans.

Yield: 2 pints

Cooking Time: 10 minutes

List of Ingredients:

- 4 cups of ice cream base, with vanilla
- ¼ cup of light brown sugar
- 1 – 2 tbsp. of bourbon
- ½ tsp. of ground cinnamon
- ¼ cup of salted pecans, roughly chopped

MMMMMMMMMMMMMMMMMMMMMMMMMMMMMM

Instructions:

1. Combine bourbon, sugar, cinnamon and base.

2. Fold in chopped pecans.

3. Taste and adjust for flavour.

4. Freeze in an airtight container for at least 6 hours.

(21) Pina Colada

What's better than a creamy version to an amazing coconut drink? This Pina Colada ice cream uses the dairy free coconut base (Vanilla Ice Cream – Dairy Free) and a little pineapple puree. It's easy to make and delicious! Top with fresh pineapples, pineapple puree, cherries, shredded coconut, nuts or whatever you like.

Yield: 2 pints

Cooking Time: 10 minutes

List of Ingredients:

- 4 cups of dairy free vanilla ice cream base
- 1 cup of pineapple puree
- 3 tbsp. of sugar

MMMMMMMMMMMMMMMMMMMMMMMMMMMMMM

Instructions:

1. Mix pineapple puree with sugar.

2. Swirl this mixture into the ice cream base.

3. Transfer to an air-tight container and freeze for 4 hours.

**Give it two minutes outside of the refrigerator before smoothing.

(22) Rum and Raisin

Rum and Raisin ice cream is great treat for adults when they've had a long way. If you're like me and you love rum and you love raisins, this flavour is perfect for you. This flavour also goes well with a spoon of caramel sauce on top.

Yield: 2 pints

Cooking Time: 20 minutes

List of Ingredients:

- 4 cups of ice cream base, with vanilla
- ½ cup of raisins
- 4 tbsp. of rum
- ½ tsp. of nutmeg

MMMMMMMMMMMMMMMMMMMMMMMMMMMMMMM

Instructions:

1. Add raisins and a tbsp. of rum to a small bowl. Cover and allow raisins to absorb rum for at least 4 hours.

2. Add remaining rum to ice cream base. Fold in raisins and nutmeg.

3. Adjust to desired taste.

4. Pour into an air tight container and freeze for at least 6 hours.

(23) Strawberry Cheesecake

Calling all cheesecake lovers! There's nothing better than combining two amazing desserts. This ice cream flavour even has the 'crust' mixed right in! It will definitely be on your favourites list. Top with fresh strawberries.

Yield: 2 pints

Cooking Time: 15 minutes

List of Ingredients:

- 3 cups of ice cream base, with vanilla
- 2 cups of Strawberry puree, with strawberry chunks
- ¼ cup of sugar
- 1 – 2 tbsp. of lemon juice
- ½ cup of cream cheese, room temperature
- ½ cup graham crackers, crushed

MMMMMMMMMMMMMMMMMMMMMMMMMMMMMM

Instructions:

1. Combine strawberry puree, lemon juice and sugar. Cook mixture over medium heat in a small sauce pan for 6 – 8 minutes. Allow to cool.

2. Whip cream cheese until smooth and stir with ice cream base.

3. Fold strawberry mixture into ice cream base to create streaks.

4. Adjust to desired taste.

5. Pour into an air tight container and top with crushed graham crackers. Freeze for at least 4 hours.

(24) Peaches and Cream

This ice cream is perfect during the summer. You get to knock two birds with one stone; take advantage of the summer peaches and beat that summer heat! This classic flavour combo is simple to make and mouth-wateringly delicious. Top with fresh peaches, soaked in cinnamon.

Yield: 2 – 2 ½ pints

Cooking Time: 10 minutes

List of Ingredients:

- 4 cups of ice cream base, without vanilla
- 4 cups of ripe peaches, pitted and cut into pieces
- ½ cup of sugar
- ½ tsp. of lemon juice

MMMMMMMMMMMMMMMMMMMMMMMMMMMMMM

Instructions:

1. Combine lemon juice, peaches and sugar in a bowl. Allow to sit for 1 hour until it becomes syrupy. Add mixture to a blender and puree mixture.

2. Add peach puree to a small sauce pan over medium heat. Allow mixture to reduce to half. About 10 minutes. Allow to cool, then refrigerate for about 2 hours.

3. Combine ice cream base and peach mixture.

4. Freeze in an airtight container for at least 6 hours.

(25) Blueberry Swirl

Blueberry swirl is a great flavour for both lovers of blueberries and non-lover of blueberry. It's that good! You get to use some fresh blueberries during blueberry season or some frozen ones in off season. Doesn't matter, it's still amazing. If your using frozen blueberries, thaw and drain them before use.

Yield: 2 – 2 ½ pints

Cooking Time: 15 minutes

List of Ingredients:

- 4 cups of ice cream base, without vanilla
- 3 cups of fresh blueberries
- 5 tbsp. of sugar
- 2 tbsp. of lemon juice

MMMMMMMMMMMMMMMMMMMMMMMMMMMMMM

Instructions:

1. Combine lemon juice, blueberries and sugar in a bowl.

2. Add blueberry mixture to a small sauce pan over medium heat. Allow mixture to reduce and blueberries to burst. About 5- 7 minutes. Allow to cool. Refrigerate for at least 1 hour.

3. Swirl mixture into ice cream base.

4. Freeze in an airtight container for at least 6 hours.

(26) Key Lime Pie

This ice cream flavour is the perfect replica to a delectable Key Lime Pie. It has the bright citrus flavour of a key lime pie and you can even mimic the graham cracker crust by sprinkling it with a crushed graham cracker mixture.

Yield: 2 pints

Cooking Time: 20 minutes

List of Ingredients:

- 4 cups of ice cream base, without vanilla
- 1 cup of cream cheese, softened
- 1 ½ tbsp. of key lime zest,
- 6 tbsp. of fresh lime juice
- Pinch of salt

MMMMMMMMMMMMMMMMMMMMMMMMMMMMMM

Instructions:

1. Beat cream cheese for about one minute, until light and creamy. Mix in ice cream base, lime zest, lime juice and salt until combined.

2. Adjust to desired taste.

3. Pour into an air tight container and freeze for at least 6 hours.

**Combine ½ cup of graham cracker crumbs, 2 tbsp. of butter and 5 tbsp. of brown sugar. Press into a microwave safe bowl and microwave for 5 - 7 minutes. Let cool and break into chunks.

(27) Strawberry Pistachio

This is perfect for you strawberry lovers out there and great dessert option after dinner. This ice cream has a delicious strawberry flavour blended with the crunch of pistachios. Top with fresh strawberries, strawberry syrup or strawberry jam.

Yield: 2 pints

Cooking Time: 10 minutes

List of Ingredients:

- 4 cups of ice cream base, without vanilla
- 1 cup of pistachios, ground and toasted
- 5 – 7 tbsp. of Strawberry puree

MMMMMMMMMMMMMMMMMMMMMMMMMMMMMM

Instructions:

1. Combine all of the ingredients.

2. Adjust to desired taste.

3. Pour into an air tight container and freeze for at least 6 hours.

(28) Rainbow

Rainbow ice cream is a fun treat to look at and to make. You can use your favourite colours to tailor it to your needs. For each colour you can also add different (edible) essential oils to make it more flavourful. Top with colourful sprinkles and candy and enjoy!

Yield: 2 pints

Cooking Time: 15 minutes

List of Ingredients:

- 4 cups of ice cream base, with vanilla
- Pink, blue, yellow and green food colouring
- Sprinkles and candy

MMMMMMMMMMMMMMMMMMMMMMMMMMMMMM

Instructions:

1. Separate ice cream base into 4 equal parts into separate bowls.

2. Add a few drops of each food colour to each portion until desired colour is achieved. Add essential oil flavouring to each if being used.

3. Pour each colour into an air tight container, one at a time. You can swirl the colours and make a pattern if you like.

4. Top with sprinkles and candy.

5. Freeze for at least 6 hours.

(29) Mint Chocolate Chip

This classic flavour has a fun green colour and is amazing. The cool flavour of mint goes great with chocolate, not to mention the crunch the chocolate chips add.

Yield: 2 pints

Cooking Time: 10 minutes

List of Ingredients:

- 4 cups of ice cream base, without vanilla
- 1 – 2 tsp. of peppermint flavour
- 1 cup of mini chocolate chips
- 1 – 2 drops of green food colouring

MMMMMMMMMMMMMMMMMMMMMMMMMMMMMM

Instructions:

1. Combine all of the ingredients. Add food colouring in 1 – 2 drop increments until desired colour is achieved.

2. Adjust to desired taste.

3. Pour into an air tight container and freeze for at least 6 hours.

(30) Chocolate Chip

This chocolate chip ice cream flavour is perfect if you are a classic vanilla lover, but you want some chocolate crunch to your ice cream. Along with mini chocolate chips, you can add crushed chocolate candy bars. Add 2 – 3 tbsp. of bourbon to make an adult version!

Yield: 2 pints

Cooking Time: 10 minutes

List of Ingredients:

- 4 cups of ice cream base, with vanilla
- ¼ cup of mini chocolate chips
- ¼ cup of chopped chocolate candy bar of your choice, such as Butterfinger

MMMMMMMMMMMMMMMMMMMMMMMMMMMMMMM

Instructions:

1. Combine all of the ingredients. If no chopped candy is used, use ½ cup of mini chocolate chips.

2. Adjust to desired texture. Add more chocolate chips if a crunchier texture is desired.

3. Pour into an air tight container and freeze for at least 6 hours.

About the Author

A native of Indianapolis, Indiana, Valeria Ray found her passion for cooking while she was studying English Literature at Oakland City University. She decided to try a cooking course with her friends and the experience changed her forever. She enrolled at the Art Institute of Indiana which offered extensive courses in the culinary Arts. Once Ray dipped her toe in the cooking world, she never looked back.

When Valeria graduated, she worked in French restaurants in the Indianapolis area until she became the head chef at one of the 5-star establishments in the area. Valeria's attention to taste and visual detail caught the eye of a local business person who expressed an interest in publishing her recipes. Valeria began her secondary career authoring cookbooks and e-books which she tackled with as much talent and gusto as her first career. Her passion for food leaps off the page of her books which have colourful anecdotes and stunning pictures of dishes she has prepared herself.

Valeria Ray lives in Indianapolis with her husband of 15 years, Tom, her daughter, Isobel and their loveable Golden Retriever, Goldy. Valeria enjoys cooking special dishes in her large, comfortable kitchen where the family gets involved in preparing meals. This successful, dynamic chef is an inspiration to culinary students and novice cooks everywhere.

●●●●●●●●● ● ● ● ● ●●●●●●●●●

Author's Afterthoughts

Thank you for Purchasing my book and taking the time to read it from front to back. I am always grateful when a reader chooses my work and I hope you enjoyed it!

With the vast selection available online, I am touched that you chose to be purchasing my work and take valuable time out of your life to read it. My hope is that you feel you made the right decision.

I very much would like to know what you thought of the book. Please take the time to write an honest and informative review on Amazon.com. Your experience and opinions will be of great benefit to me and those readers looking to make an informed choice.

With much thanks,

Valeria Ray

Printed in Great Britain
by Amazon

12322865R00043